Pebble™

Grassland Animals

Red Foxes

by Patricia J. Murphy

Consulting Editor: Gail Saunders-Smith, Ph.D.
Consultant: Marsha A. Sovada, Ph.D., Research Wildlife Biologist
Northern Prairie Wildlife Research Center, U.S. Geological Survey
Jamestown, North Dakota

Capstone
press
Mankato, Minnesota

Pebble Books are published by Capstone Press
151 Good Counsel Drive, P.O. Box 669, Mankato, Minnesota 56002
www.capstonepress.com

1 2 3 4 5 6 09 08 07 06 05 04

Library of Congress Cataloging-in-Publication Data
Murphy, Patricia J., 1963–
    Red foxes / by Patricia J. Murphy.
    p. cm.—(Grassland animals)
    Summary: Simple text and photographs introduce red foxes and their
grasslands habitat.
    Includes bibliographical references (p. 23) and index.
    ISBN 0-7368-2074-4 (hardcover)
    1. Red fox—Juvenile literature. [1. Red fox. 2. Foxes. 3. Grasslands.]
I. Title. II. Series.
QL737.C22M792 2004
599.775—dc22   2003013419

Note to Parents and Teachers

The Grassland Animals series supports national science standards
related to life science. This book describes and illustrates red foxes.
The photographs support early readers in understanding the text.
The repetition of words and phrases helps early readers learn new
words. This book also introduces early readers to subject-specific
vocabulary words, which are defined in the Glossary. Early readers
may need assistance to read some words and to use the Table of
Contents, Glossary, Read More, Internet Sites, and Index/Word List
sections of the book.

Table of Contents

Red Foxes. 5

Where Red Foxes Live 11

What Red Foxes Do 15

Glossary 22

Read More 23

Internet Sites 23

Index/Word List 24

4

Red Foxes

Red foxes are mammals in the dog family. Red foxes have pointed ears and long snouts.

Red foxes have long red, white, and black fur. Their long, bushy tails have white tips.

Red foxes have strong jaws and sharp teeth. They have long legs and sharp claws.

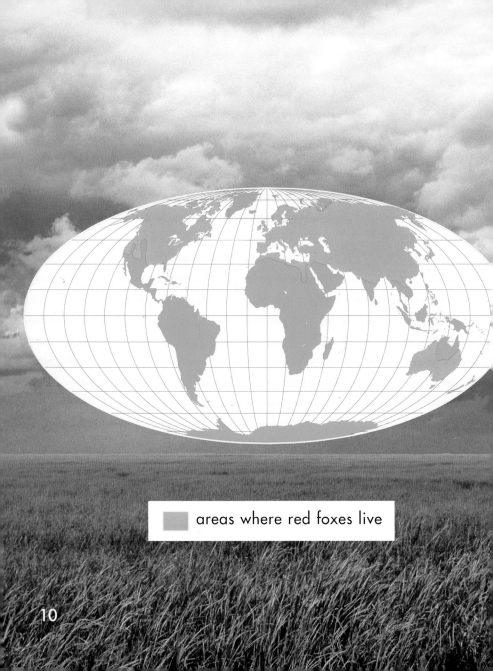

areas where red foxes live

Where Red Foxes Live

Red foxes roam grasslands. Grasslands are large open areas of grass.

Red foxes live
in family groups.

14

What Red Foxes Do

Red foxes pounce on their prey. They hunt small mammals and insects. Red foxes often store their extra food.

Red foxes run fast
to escape predators.
Coyotes and cougars
hunt red foxes.

Red foxes raise their kits in dens.

Red foxes sleep outside. Their bushy tails keep them warm.

Glossary

claw—a hard, curved nail on a foot of an animal; red foxes have sharp claws on their front paws that they use to dig.

den—a home of a wild animal; red foxes find dens to give birth and raise young red foxes.

kit—a young fox; female foxes can have four to nine kits at one time.

mammal—a warm-blooded animal that has a backbone; mammals have fur or hair; female mammals feed milk to their young.

predator—an animal that hunts other animals

prey—an animal that is hunted by another animal for food; red foxes eat small mammals, insects, and earthworms.

snout—the long front part of an animal's face; the snout includes the nose, mouth, and jaws.

Read More

Gentle, Victor, and Janet Perry. *Red Foxes.* Wild Dogs. Milwaukee: Gareth Stevens, 2002.

Greenaway, Theresa. *Wolves, Wild Dogs, and Foxes.* The Secret World Of. Austin, Texas: Raintree Steck-Vaughn Publishers, 2001.

Whitledge, Doran and Jane. *Red Foxes.* Northern Trek. North Mankato, Minn.: Smart Apple Media, 2002.

Internet Sites

FactHound offers a safe, fun way to find Internet sites related to this book. All of the sites on FactHound have been researched by our staff.

Here's how:

1. Visit *www.facthound.com*
2. Type in this special code **0736820744** for age-appropriate sites. Or enter a search word related to this book for a more general search.
3. Click on the **Fetch It** button.

FactHound will fetch the best sites for you!

Index/Word List

claws, 9
dens, 19
dog, 5
ears, 5
escape, 17
family, 13
fur, 7
grasslands, 11

hunt, 15, 17
jaws, 9
kits, 19
legs, 9
mammals,
  5, 15
pounce, 15
predators, 17

prey, 15
raise, 19
sleep, 21
snouts, 5
store, 15
tails, 7, 21
teeth, 9

Word Count: 113
Early-Intervention Level: 13

Editorial Credits
Martha E. H. Rustad, editor; Patrick Dentinger, designer; Scott Thoms,
    photo researcher; Karen Risch, product planning editor

Photo Credits
Corbis, 6, 10; Darrell Gulin, 4; John Conrad, 14
Corel, 8, 20
DigitalVision, 1
Erwin and Peggy Bauer, 12, 16
Fi Rust/GeoIMAGERY, cover
Tom Stack & Associates/Thomas Kitchin, 18